WORLD HISTORY BOOK

WHAT HAPPENED IN 1995

THE YEAR YOU WERE BORN

VINTAGE HISTORICAL EVENTS

Major Events :

Jan 1 : The World Trade Organization is established to replace the General Agreement on Tariffs and Trade.

Jan 1 : Austria, Finland and Sweden join the European Union.

Jan 9 : Valeri Polyakov completes 366 days in space while aboard the Mir space station, breaking a duration record.

Jan 17 : The 6.9 Mw Great Hanshin earthquake strikes the southern Hyōgo Prefecture of Japan with a maximum Shindo of VII, leaving 5,502–6,434 people dead, and 251,301–310,000 displaced.

Jan 25 : A rocket launched from the space exploration centre at Andøya, Norway, is briefly interpreted by the Russians as an incoming attack.

Jan 31 : Mexican peso crisis: U.S. President Bill Clinton invokes emergency powers to extend a $20 billion loan to help Mexico avert financial collapse.

Major Events :

Feb 13 : Twenty-one Bosnian Serb commanders are charged with genocide and crimes against humanity in the United Nations' International Criminal Tribunal for the former Yugoslavia, a tribunal on human rights violations during the Wars in the Balkans.

Feb 21 : Steve Fossett lands in Leader, Saskatchewan, Canada, becoming the first person to make a solo flight across the Pacific Ocean in a balloon.

Feb 25 : The Amazon Cooperation Treaty Organization is formed.

Feb 26 : The United Kingdom's oldest investment banking firm, Barings Bank, collapses after securities broker Nick Leeson loses $1.4 billion by speculating on the Tokyo Stock Exchange.

Mar 1 : Julio María Sanguinetti is sworn in as President of Uruguay for his second term.

Mar 1 : Polish Prime Minister Waldemar Pawlak resigns from Parliament and is replaced by ex-communist Józef Oleksy.

Major Events :

Mar 3 : United Nations Operation in Somalia II, the United Nations peacekeeping mission in Somalia, ends.

Mar 14 : Astronaut Norman Thagard becomes the first American to ride into space aboard a Russian launch vehicle , lifting off from the Baikonur Cosmodrome in Kazakhstan.

Mar 20 : Members of the doomsday cult Aum Shinrikyo carry out the Tokyo subway sarin attack, killing 14 people and leading to over a thousand injured. The attack remains the deadliest terrorist incident in Japanese history.

Mar 22 : Cosmonaut Valeri Polyakov returns after setting a record for 438 days in outer space.

Mar 25 : Boxer Mike Tyson is released from prison after serving nearly 3 years.

Mar 26 : The Schengen Agreement, easing cross-border travel, goes into effect in several European countries.

Mar 31 : TAROM Flight 371 from Bucharest to Brussels crashes shortly after takeoff killing all 60 people on board.

Major Events :

Mar 31 : American singer Selena is murdered by her fan club president, Yolanda Saldívar.

Apr 7 : First Chechen War – Samashki massacre Russian paramilitary troops begin a massacre of at least 250 civilians in Samashki, Chechnya.

Apr 19 : Oklahoma City bombing: 168 people, including eight federal Marshals and 19 children, are killed at the Alfred P. Murrah Federal Building and 680 are wounded by a bomb set off by Timothy McVeigh and one of his accomplices, Terry Nichols.

Apr 28 : In Daegu, South Korea, a gas explosion at a subway construction site kills 101 people, mostly teenage schoolboys.

Apr 30 : The United States government stops funding the NSFNET, making the Internet a wholly privatized system.

May 7 : Jacques Chirac is elected president of France.

Major Events :

May 10 : At Vaal Reefs gold mine in Orkney, a runaway locomotive falls into a lift shaft onto an ascending cage and causes it to plunge 1,500 feet to the bottom of the 6,900-foot deep shaft, killing 104.

May 11 : More than 170 countries agree to extend the Nuclear Nonproliferation Treaty indefinitely and without conditions.

May 12 : Mia Martini is found dead.

May 13 : The 6.6 Mw Western Macedonia earthquake strikes northwestern Greece with a maximum Mercalli intensity of VIII , injuring 25 and causing $450 million in damage.

May 14 : The Dalai Lama proclaims 6-year-old Gedhun Choekyi Nyima as the 11th reincarnation of the Panchen Lama.

May 16 : Following the Tokyo subway sarin attack two months earlier, Japanese police besiege the headquarters of Aum Shinrikyo near Mount Fuji and arrest cult leader Shoko Asahara. Further police operations result in over two hundred arrests and thirteen members of the cult, including Asahara, are sentenced to death.

Major Events :

May 24 : AFC Ajax wins the UEFA Champions League at the Ernst Happel Stadium in Vienna by defeating A.C. Milan 1–0.

May 28 : The 7.0 Mw Neftegorsk earthquake strikes northern Sakhalin Island in Russia with a maximum Mercalli intensity of IX , leaving 1,967 people dead and 750 injured.

Jun 2 : Mrkonjić Grad incident: A United States Air Force F-16 piloted by Captain Scott O'Grady is shot down over Bosnia and Herzegovina while patrolling the NATO no-fly zone. O'Grady is rescued by U.S. Marines six days later.

Jun 2 : Waffen-SS Hauptsturmführer Erich Priebke is extradited from Argentina to Italy.

Jun 6 : U.S. astronaut Norman Thagard breaks NASA's space endurance record of 14 days, 1 hour and 16 minutes, aboard the Russian space station Mir.

Jun 6 : The Constitutional Court of South Africa abolishes capital punishment in South Africa in the case of S v Makwanyane and Another.

Major Events :

Jun 13 : French President Jacques Chirac announces the resumption of nuclear tests in French Polynesia.

Jun 16 : The IOC selects Salt Lake City to host the 2002 Winter Olympics.

Jun 22 : Japanese police rescue 365 hostages from a hijacked All Nippon Airways Flight 857 at Hakodate airport. The hijacker was armed with a knife and demanded the release of Shoko Asahara.

Jun 24 : South Africa wins the Rugby World Cup.

Jun 29 : Lisa Clayton completes her 10-month solo circumnavigation from the Northern Hemisphere.

Jun 29 : Space Shuttle Atlantis docks with the Russian Mir space station for the first time.

Jul 1 : In response to UNSCOM's evidence, Iraq admits for first time the existence of an offensive biological weapons program, but denies weaponization.

Major Events :

Jul 4 : Prime Minister of the United Kingdom John Major is re-elected as leader of the Conservative Party.

Jul 9 : 125 civilians are killed in Navaly as result of bombing by the Sri Lanka Air Force.

Jul 10 : Burmese dissident Aung San Suu Kyi is freed from house arrest.

Jul 11 : Units of the Army of Republika Srpska, under the command of General Ratko Mladić, enter Srebrenica with little resistance from Dutch peacekeepers of the United Nations Protection Force, going on to kill thousands of Bosniak men and boys and rape many women.

Jul 11 : President Clinton announces the restoration of United States–Vietnam relations twenty years after the Vietnam War.

Aug 4 : Croatian forces, with the cooperation of the ARBiH, launch Operation Storm against rebel forces of the Republic of Serbian Krajina, which subsequently ceases to exist as a political entity.

Major Events :

Aug 7 : The Chilean government declares state of emergency in the southern half of the country in response to an event of intense, cold, wind, rain and snowfall known as the White Earthquake.

Aug 16 : Bermudans reject independence in a referendum.

Aug 29 : Eduard Shevardnadze, the Georgian head of state, survives an assassination attempt in Tbilisi.

Aug 30 : The NATO bombing campaign against Bosnian Serb artillery positions begins in Bosnia and Herzegovina, continuing into September. At the same time, ARBiH forces begin an offensive against the Bosnian Serb Army around Sarajevo, central Bosnia and Bosnian Krajina.

Sep 3 : Bay is founded by Pierre Omidyar.

Sep 4 : The Fourth World Conference on Women in Beijing with over 4,750 delegates from 181 countries in attendance.

Sep 6 : NATO air strikes against Bosnian Serb forces continue, after repeated attempts at a solution to the Bosnian War fail.

Major Events :

Sep 9 : Sony enters the video game market with the release of the PlayStation.

Sep 19 : The Washington Post and The New York Times publish the Unabomber manifesto.

Sep 26 : The trial against former Italian Prime Minister Giulio Andreotti, who is accused of Mafia connections, begins.

Sep 27 : Bob Denard's mercenaries capture President Said Mohammed Djohor of the Comoros; the local army does not resist.

Oct 3 : O. J. Simpson is found not guilty of double murder for the deaths of former wife Nicole Brown Simpson and Ronald Goldman.

Oct 5 : Tansu Çiller of DYP forms the new government of Turkey.

Oct 6 : Michel Mayor and Didier Queloz announce the discovery of 51 Pegasi b, the first confirmed extrasolar planet orbiting an ordinary main-sequence star.

Oct 16 : The Million Man March is held in Washington, D.C. The event was conceived by Nation of Islam leader Louis Farrakhan.

Major Events :

Oct 17 : French woman Jeanne Calment reaches the confirmed age of 120 years and 238 days, making her the oldest person ever recorded.

Oct 24 : A total solar eclipse is visible from Iran, India, Thailand, and Southeast Asia.

Oct 25 : A commuter train slams into a school bus in Fox River Grove, Illinois, killing seven students.

Oct 26 : An avalanche hits the village Flateyri in Iceland, killing 20 people. It was the second of two deadly avalanches that occurred in Iceland during the calendar year.

Oct 28 : A fire in Baku Metro, Azerbaijan, kills 289 passengers, becoming the world's worst subway disaster.

Oct 30 : Quebec independentists narrowly lose a referendum for a mandate to negotiate independence from Canada.

Oct 30 : Tansu Çiller of DYP forms the new government of Turkey.

Nov 1 : The last signal is received from NASA's Pioneer 11 spacecraft.

Major Events :

Nov 1 : Participants in the Yugoslav Wars begin negotiations at the Wright-Patterson Air Force Base in Dayton, Ohio.

Nov 2 : The Supreme Court of Argentina orders the extradition of ex-S.S. captain Erich Priebke.

Nov 4 : Israeli Prime Minister Yitzhak Rabin is assassinated at a peace rally in Tel Aviv.

Nov 7 : Typhoon Angela leaves the Philippines and Vietnam devastated, with 882 deaths and US$315 million in damage. The typhoon was the strongest ever to strike the Philippines in 25 years, with wind speeds of 130 mph and gusts of 180 mph.

Nov 12 : The Millbrook Commonwealth Action Programme, a programme to implement the Harare Declaration, is announced by the Commonwealth Heads of Government.

Nov 16 : A United Nations tribunal charges Radovan Karadžić and Ratko Mladić with genocide during the Bosnian War.

Major Events :

Nov 19 : A car bomb explosion outside the Egyptian Embassy in Islamabad, Pakistan, destroyed the face of the building, killed at least 13 people and wounded dozens more.

Nov 21 : The Dayton Agreement to end the Bosnian War is reached at Wright-Patterson Air Force Base near Dayton, Ohio.

Nov 22 : The 7.3 Mw Gulf of Aqaba earthquake shakes the Sinai Peninsula and Saudi Arabia region with a maximum Mercalli intensity of VIII , killing eight and injuring 30, and generating a non-destructive tsunami.

Nov 22 : The first-ever full-length computer-animated feature film, Toy Story, is released by Pixar and Walt Disney Pictures.

Nov 28 : Twenty-seven nations sign the Barcelona Treaty, creating the Union for the Mediterranean.

Nov 30 : Operation Desert Storm officially ends.

Dec 3 : Strikes paralyze France's public sector.

Major Events :

Dec 6 : The United States Food and Drug Administration approved Saquinavir, the first protease inhibitor to treat HIV/AIDS. Within 2 years of its approval, annual deaths from AIDS in the United States fell from over 50,000 to approximately 18,000.

Dec 7 : NASA's Galileo Probe enters Jupiter's atmosphere.

Dec 8 : Five-year-old Gyaincain Norbu is enthroned as the 11th reincarnation of the Panchen Lama at Tashilhunpo Monastery.

Dec 9 : Godzilla vs. Destoroyah is released by Toho Studios, the last Godzilla incarnation era of Godzilla films.

Dec 14 : The Dayton Agreement is signed in Paris, officially ending the Bosnian War.

Dec 16 : Iraqi scuba divers, under the direction of the United Nations Special Commission, dredge the Tigris near Baghdad. The divers find over 200 prohibited Russian-made missile instruments and components.

Major Events :

Dec 20 : American Airlines Flight 965 crashes into a mountain near Buga, Valle del Cauca, Colombia, killing 160 of the 164 on board.

Dec 20 : NATO begins peacekeeping in Bosnia.

Dec 30 : The lowest ever United Kingdom temperature of −27.2 °C is recorded at Altnaharra in the Scottish Highlands. This equals the record set at Braemar, Aberdeenshire in 1895 and 1982.

Sports Events :

American football :

Super Bowl XXIX :
The San Francisco 49ers (NFC) won 49–26 over the San Diego Chargers (AFC)
Location: Joe Robbie Stadium
Attendance: 74,107
MVP: Steve Young, QB (San Francisco)

The World League of American Football is resumed after 2 years without play. Frankfurt Galaxy win the World Bowl 26–22 over the Amsterdam Admirals.

Orange Bowl (1994 season):
The Nebraska Cornhuskers won 24–17 over the Miami Hurricanes to win the national championship

Baseball :

World Series :
Atlanta Braves won 4 games to 2 over the Cleveland Indians. The Series MVP was Tom Glavine, Atlanta

Cal Ripken Jr. breaks Lou Gehrig's record of playing 2130 consecutive games.

Sports Events :

California Angels lose a 13-game lead over the Seattle Mariners, and lose the division title in a one-game playoff.

Basketball :

NCAA Men's Basketball Championship :
UCLA wins 89–78 over Arkansas, giving the Bruins their first National College Basketball Championship in 20 years, and 11th overall.

NBA Finals :
Houston Rockets win 4 games to 0 over the Orlando Magic

Pan American Games held in Mar del Plata, Argentina.* May 6 – Oscar De La Hoya scored a second-round TKO in Las Vegas over Rafael Ruelas to retain his World Lightweight Championship.

Golf :

Men's professional :
U.S. Open :
Corey Pavin

Men's amateur :
U.S. Amateur - Tiger Woods

Sports Events :

Women's professional :
U.S. Women's Open :
Annika Sörenstam

Harness racing :

Pacing Triple Crown races :
Cane Pace - Mattgrilla Gorilla
Little Brown Jug - Nick's Fantasy
Messenger Stakes - David's Pass

Trotting Triple Crown races :
Hambletonian - Tagliabue Yonkers Trot -
Kentucky Futurity - CR Trackmaster

Horse racing :

Steeplechases :
Cheltenham Gold Cup – Master Oats
Grand National – Royal Athlete

Flat races :
Triple Crown races :
Kentucky Derby – Thunder Gulch
Preakness Stakes – Timber Country
Belmont Stakes – Thunder Gulch

Sports Events :

Ice hockey :

Art Ross Trophy as the NHL's leading scorer during the regular season: Jaromir Jagr, Pittsburgh Penguins

Hart Memorial Trophy :
For the NHL's Most Valuable Player: Eric Lindros, Philadelphia Flyers

Stanley Cup :
New Jersey Devils win 4 games to 0 over the Detroit Red Wings

Lacrosse :

Major Indoor Lacrosse League Championship: The Philadelphia Wings win 15–14 over the Rochester Knighthawks after overtime.

World Snooker Championship :
Stephen Hendry beats Nigel Bond 18-9

World rankings :
Stephen Hendry remains world number one for 1995/96

Sports Events :

Taekwondo :

World Championships held in Manila, Philippines

Tennis :

US Open :
Pete Sampras

US Open :
Steffi Graf

Davis Cup :
The USA wins 3–2 over Russia.

Fed Cup :
Spain wins 3–2 over the USA in the first Fed Cup to bear that name, and the first to employ a Davis Cup-style format.

Sports Events :

Yacht racing :

New Zealand wins its first America's Cup as Black Magic, of the Royal New Zealand Yacht Squadron, beats defender Young America, from the San Diego Yacht Club, 5 races to 0

Awards :

Associated Press Male Athlete of the Year : Cal Ripken Jr., Major League Baseball

Associated Press Female Athlete of the Year : Rebecca Lobo, College basketball

Sports Events :

Premier League Standings :

1- Blackburn Rovers (C) 89 Pts
2- Manchester United 88 Pts
3- Nottingham Forest 77 Pts
4- Liverpool 74 Pts
5- Leeds United 73 Pts
6- Newcastle United 72 Pts
7- Tottenham Hotspur 62 Pts
8- Queens Park Rangers 60 Pts
9- Wimbledon 56 Pts
10- Southampton 54 Pts
11- Chelsea 54 Pts
12- Arsenal 51 Pts
13- Sheffield Wednesday 51 Pts
14- West Ham United 50 Pts
15- Everton 50 Pts
16- Coventry City 50 Pts
17- Manchester City 49 Pts
18- Aston Villa 48 Pts
19- Crystal Palace (R) 45 Pts
20- Norwich City (R) 43 Pts
21- Leicester City (R) 29 Pts
22- Ipswich Town (R) 27 Pts

Top Goalscorer :

Alan Shearer (Blackburn Rovers) : 34 Goals

Sports Events :

1st Division League Standings :

1- Middlesbrough 82 Pts
2- Reading 79 Pts
3- Bolton Wanderers 77 Pts
4- Wolverhampton Wanderers 76 Pts
5- Tranmere Rovers 76 Pts
6- Barnsley 72 Pts
7- Watford 70 Pts
8- Sheffield United 68 Pts
9- Derby County 66 Pts
10- Grimsby Town 65 Pts
11- Stoke City 63 Pts
12- Millwall 62 Pts
13- Southend United 62 Pts
14- Oldham Athletic 61 Pts
15- Charlton Athletic 59 Pts
16- Luton Town 58 Pts
17- Port Vale 58 Pts
18- Portsmouth 58 Pts
19- West Bromwich Albion 58 Pts
20- Sunderland 54 Pts
21- Swindon Town 48 Pts
22- Burnley 46 Pts

Top Goalscorer :

Leading goalscorer: John Aldridge (Tranmere Rovers) : 24 Goals

Sports Events :

2nd Division League Standings :

1- Birmingham City 89 Pts
2- Brentford 85 Pts
3- Crewe Alexandra 83 Pts
4- Bristol Rovers 82 Pts
5- Huddersfield Town 81 Pts
6- Wycombe Wanderers 78 Pts
7- Oxford United 75 Pts
8- Hull City 74 Pts
9- York City 72 Pts
10- Swansea City 71 Pts
11- Stockport County 65 Pts
12- Blackpool 64 Pts
13- Wrexham 63 Pts
14- Bradford City 60 Pts
15- Peterborough United 60 Pts
16- Brighton & Hove Albion 59 Pts
17- Rotherham United 56 Pts
18- Shrewsbury Town 53 Pts
19- AFC Bournemouth 50 Pts
20- Cambridge United 48 Pts
21- Plymouth Argyle 46 Pts
22- Cardiff City 38 Pts

Top Goalscorer :

Leading goalscorer: Gary Bennett (Wrexham) : 29 Goals

Sports Events :

3rd Division League Standings :

1- Carlisle United 91 Pts
2- Walsall 83 Pts
3- Chesterfield 81 Pts
4- Bury 80 Pts
5- Preston North End 67 Pts
6- Mansfield Town 65 Pts
7- Scunthorpe United 62 Pts
8- Fulham 62 Pts
9- Doncaster Rovers 61 Pts
10- Colchester United 58 Pts
11- Barnet 56 Pts
12- Lincoln City 56 Pts
13- Torquay United 55 Pts
14- Wigan Athletic 52 Pts
15- Rochdale 50 Pts
16- Hereford United 49 Pts
17- Northampton Town 44 Pts
18- Hartlepool United 43 Pts
19- Gillingham 41 Pts
20- Darlington 41 Pts
21- Scarborough 34 Pts
22- Exeter City 34 Pts

Top Goalscorer :

Dougie Freedman (Barnet) : 24 Goals

Sports Events :

FA Cup final :

Everton 1-0 Manchester United at Wembley Stadium, London.

League Cup :

Liverpool were winners of the league Cup after a 2–1 final win over Bolton Wanderers.

1st Division Scottish League Standings :

1- Rangers (C) 69 Pts
2- Motherwell 54 Pts
3- Hibernian 53 Pts
4- Celtic 51 Pts
5- Falkirk 48 Pts
6- Heart of Midlothian 43 Pts
7- Kilmarnock 43 Pts
8- Partick Thistle 43 Pts
9- Aberdeen (O) 41 Pts
10- Dundee United (R) 36 Pts

Sports Events :

Scottish Cup :

Celtic were winners of the Scottish Cup after a 1–0 final win over Airdrieonians.

2nd Division Scottish League Standings :

1- Greenock Morton 64 Pts

2- Dumbarton 60 Pts

3- Stirling Albion 58 Pts

4- Stenhousemuir 56 Pts

5- Berwick Rangers 55 Pts

6- Clyde 52 Pts

7- Queen of the South 44 Pts

8- East Fife 43 Pts

9- Meadowbank Thistle 35 Pts

10- Brechin City 24 Pts

Sports Events :

League Cup :

Raith Rovers were winners of the League Cup after
a 2 – 2 (a.e.t.)(6 – 5 pen.) final
win over Celtic

Irish League Standings :

1- Crusaders (C) 67 Pts
2- Glenavon 60 Pts
3- Portadown 50 Pts
4- Ards 50 Pts
5- Glentoran 50 Pts
6- Cliftonville 50 Pts
7- Coleraine (R) 49 Pts
8- Linfield 44 Pts
9- Omagh Town (R) 42 Pts
10- Distillery (R) 42 Pts
11- Bangor 38 Pts
12- Ballymena United (R) 29 Pts
13- Carrick Rangers (R) 25 Pts
14- Ballyclare Comrades (R) 24 Pts
15- Newry Town (R) 21 Pts
16- Larne (R) 13 Pts

Celebrity Births :

Jan 1 : Poppy, American musician and model.

Jan 4 : María Isabel, Spanish singer.

Jan 9 : Nicola Peltz, American actress.

Jan 12 : Alessio Romagnoli, Italian footballer.

Jan 16 : Takumi Minamino, Japanese footballer.

Jan 19 : Mathieu van der Poel, Dutch bicycle racer.

Jan 20 : Joey Badass, American rapper.

Jan 24 : Callan McAuliffe, Australian actor.

Jan 30 : Danielle Campbell, American actress.

Jan 31 : Nina Sublatti, Georgian singer and model.

Feb 4 : Pione Sisto, South Sudanese-Danish footballer.

Feb 5 : Adnan Januzaj, Belgian footballer.

Feb 6 : Leon Goretzka, German footballer.

Feb 8 : Joshua Kimmich, German footballer.

Celebrity Births :

Feb 9 : Mario Pašalić, Croatian footballer.

Feb 10 : Naby Keïta, Guinean footballer.

Feb 11 : Milan Škriniar, Slovak footballer.

Feb 15 : Megan Thee Stallion, American rapper.

Feb 16 : Denzel Curry, American rapper.

Feb 17 : Madison Keys, American tennis player.

Feb 18 : Mikhail Kolyada, Russian figure skater.

Feb 23 : Andrew Wiggins, Canadian basketball player.

Feb 27 : Sergej Milinković-Savić, Serbian footballer.

Mar 2 : Mats Møller Dæhli, Norwegian footballer.

Mar 7 : Haley Lu Richardson, American actress.

Mar 8 : Keita Baldé, Senegalese footballer.

Mar 9 : Cierra Ramirez, American actress and singer.

Celebrity Births :

Mar 10 : Zach LaVine, American basketball player.

Mar 13 : Mikaela Shiffrin, American skier.

Mar 15 : Jabari Parker, American basketball player.

Mar 19 : Julia Montes, Filipina actress.

Mar 23 : Ester Ledecká, Czech winter athlete.

Mar 25 : Carlos Vinícius, Brazilian footballer.

Mar 27 : Zaur Uguev, Russian freestyle wrestler.

Mar 30 : Tao Geoghegan Hart, British cyclist.

Apr 3 : Adrien Rabiot, French footballer.

Apr 17 : Wheein, South Korean singer and songwriter.

Apr 18 : Divock Origi, Belgian footballer.

Apr 23 : Gigi Hadid, American fashion model.

Apr 24 : Kehlani, American singer.

Apr 26 : Daniel Padilla, Filipino actor.

Celebrity Births :

Apr 28 : Melanie Martinez, American singer.

May 1 : Radhika Madan, Indian actress and dancer.

May 2 : Yook Sung-jae, South Korean singer and actor.

May 6 : Marko Pjaca, Croatian footballer.

May 10 : Missy Franklin, American swimmer.

May 11 : Shira Haas, Israeli actress.

May 14 : Kelly Gale, Swedish model.

May 15 : Ksenia Sitnik, Belarusian singer.

May 23 : Eula Caballero, Filipina actress.

May 25 : José Luis Gayà, Spanish footballer.

May 29 : Nicolas Pépé, Ivorian footballer.

Jun 4 : Willie Rioli, Australian football player.

Jun 13 : Petra Vlhová, Slovak alpine skier.

Jun 16 : Joseph Schooling, Singaporean swimmer.

Celebrity Births :

Jun 21 : Darko Velkovski, Macedonian footballer.

Jun 22 : Ádám Borbély, Hungarian handball player.

Jun 23 : Eva Lazzaro, Australian actress.

Jun 24 : Abdel Fadel Suanon, Beninese footballer.

Jun 25 : Wilhem Belocian, French sprinter.

Jun 26 : Natsuhiko Watanabe, Japanese footballer.

Jun 28 : Kåre Hedebrant, Swedish actor.

Jun 30 : Marina Ruy Barbosa, Brazilian actress.

Jul 1 : Krzysztof Piątek, Polish footballer.

Jul 2 : Ryan Murphy, American competitive swimmer.

Jul 3 : Emircan Koşut, Turkish basketball player.

Jul 4 : Álex Berenguer, Spanish footballer.

Jul 5 : Hyuk, South Korean singer and actor.

Celebrity Births :

Jul 9 : Georgie Henley, English actress.

Jul 10 : Ada Hegerberg, Norwegian footballer.

Jul 12 : Luke Shaw, English footballer.

Jul 13 : Dante Exum, Australian basketball player.

Jul 14 : Serge Gnabry, German footballer.

Jul 15 : Vivianne Miedema, Dutch football player.

Jul 16 : Torstein Træen, Norwegian racing cyclist.

Jul 19 : Manuel Akanji, Swiss footballer.

Jul 24 : Kyle Kuzma, American basketball player.

Jul 30 : Hirving Lozano, Mexican footballer.

Aug 1 : Madison Cawthorn, American politician.

Aug 2 : Kristaps Porziņģis, Latvian basketball player.

Aug 4 : Jessica Sanchez, American singer.

Aug 5 : Pierre-Emile Højbjerg, Danish footballer.

Celebrity Births :

Aug 12 : Sara Ali Khan, Indian actress.

Aug 13 : Presnel Kimpembe, French footballer.

Aug 15 : Chief Keef, American rapper.

Aug 16 : James Young, American basketball player.

Aug 17 : Gracie Gold, American figure skater.

Aug 22 : Dua Lipa, English singer.

Aug 24 : Justine Skye, American singer.

Aug 26 : Gracie Dzienny, American actress.

Aug 27 : Sergey Sirotkin, Russian racing driver.

Aug 28 : Andreas Wellinger, German ski jumper.

Aug 29 : Gud, Swedish DJ and producer.

Sep 1 : Munir El Haddadi, Spanish footballer.

Sep 3 : Niklas Süle, German footballer.

Sep 6 : Bertrand Traoré, Burkinabé footballer.

Celebrity Births :

Sep 8 : Julian Weigl, German footballer.

Sep 12 : Ryan Potter, American actor.

Sep 16 : Aaron Gordon, American basketball player.

Sep 17 : Patrick Mahomes, American football player.

Sep 20 : Laura Dekker, Dutch sailor.

Sep 22 : Nayeon, South Korean singer.

Sep 23 : Eli Dershwitz, American fencer.

Sep 29 : Mozzik, Albanian rapper.

Oct 1 : Scott Helman, Canadian singer-songwriter.

Oct 4 : Jabrill Peppers, American football player.

Oct 5 : Kim A-lim South Korean golfer.

Oct 9 : Kenny Tete, Dutch footballer.

Oct 13 : Jimin, South Korean singer.

Oct 15 : Billy Unger, American actor and musician.

Celebrity Births :

Oct 17 : Queen Naija, American singer.

Oct 21 : Doja Cat, American singer and rapper.

Oct 25 : Conchita Campbell, Canadian actress.

Oct 28 : Mia Wray, Australian pop musician.

Nov 1 : Nour El Sherbini, Egyptian squash player.

Nov 2 : Rafael Vitti, Brazilian actor, musician and poet.

Nov 3 : Kelly Catlin, American racing cyclist (d. 2019).

Nov 6 : André Silva, Portuguese footballer.

Nov 13 : Oliver Stummvoll, Austrian model.

Nov 17 : Elise Mertens, Belgian tennis player.

Nov 18 : Ihsan Maulana Mustofa, Indonesian badminton player.

Nov 19 : Vanessa Axente, Hungarian fashion model.

Nov 20 : Timothy Cheruiyot, Kenyan athlete.

Celebrity Births :

Nov 22 : Katherine McNamara, American actress.

Nov 28 : Tin Jedvaj, Croatian footballer.

Nov 29 : Laura Marano, American actress and singer.

Dec 4 : Dina Asher-Smith, British sprinter.

Dec 5 : Anthony Martial, French footballer.

Dec 6 : Joy Gruttmann, German singer.

Dec 9 : McKayla Maroney, American gymnast.

Dec 14 : Yulia Belokobylskaya, Russian gymnast.

Dec 15 : Yoshihide Kiryū, Japanese sprinter.

Dec 18 : Lim Na-young, South Korean singer.

Dec 27 : Carlos Cuevas, Spanish actor.

Dec 29 : Ross Lynch, American actor.

Dec 30 : V, South Korean singer.

Dec 31 : Gabby Douglas, American gymnast

Celebrity Deaths :

Jan 1 : Eugene Wigner, Hungarian physicist (b. 1902).

Jan 1 : Fred West, English serial killer (b. 1941).

Jan 2 : Nancy Kelly, American actress (b. 1921).

Jan 7 : Murray Rothbard, American economist (b. 1926).

Jan 8 : Carlos Monzón, Argentine boxer (b. 1942).

Jan 9 : Peter Cook, English comedian and writer (b. 1937).

Jan 11 : Josef Gingold, Russian-American violinist (b. 1909).

Jan 17 : Miguel Torga, Portuguese writer (b. 1907).

Jan 20 : Mehdi Bazargan, 46th Prime Minister of Iran (b. 1907).

Jan 22 : Rose Kennedy, American philanthropist (b. 1890).

Jan 25 : John Smith, American actor (b. 1931).

Celebrity Deaths :

Jan 25 : William Sylvester, American actor (b. 1922).

Jan 31 : George Stibitz, American computational engineer (b. 1904).

Feb 2 : Tikvah Alper, South African scientist (b. 1909).

Feb 2 : Fred Perry, English tennis champion (b. 1909).

Feb 4 : Patricia Highsmith, American author (b. 1921).

Feb 5 : Doug McClure, American actor (b. 1935).

Feb 6 : James Merrill, American poet (b. 1926).

Feb 6 : Art Taylor, American jazz drummer (b. 1929).

Feb 9 : David Wayne, American actor (b. 1914).

Feb 12 : Robert Bolt, English dramatist (b. 1924).

Feb 13 : Alberto Burri, Italian artist (b. 1915).

Feb 19 : John Howard, American actor (b. 1913).

Celebrity Deaths :

Feb 22 : Ed Flanders, American actor (b. 1934).

Feb 23 : James Herriot, English veterinarian and author (b. 1916).

Feb 24 : Hideko Maehata, Japanese swimmer (b. 1914).

Feb 26 : Jack Clayton, British film director (b. 1921).

Mar 1 : Georges J. F. Köhler, German biologist (b. 1946).

Mar 1 : Vladislav Listyev, Russian journalist (b. 1956).

Mar 8 : Ingo Schwichtenberg, German drummer (b. 1965).

Mar 9 : Yisrael Galil, Israeli firearm designer (b. 1923).

Mar 10 : Ovidi Montllor, Spanish singer and actor (b. 1942).

Mar 14 : William Alfred Fowler, American physicist (b. 1911).

Celebrity Deaths :

Mar 17 : Rick Aviles, American actor (b. 1952).

Mar 20 : Sidney Kingsley, American dramatist (b. 1906).

Mar 23 : Davie Cooper, Scottish footballer (b. 1956).

Mar 25 : James Samuel Coleman, American sociologist (b. 1926).

Mar 26 : Eazy-E, American rapper and record producer (b. 1964).

Mar 31 : Selena, American singer (b. 1971).

Apr 2 : Hannes Alfvén, Swedish chemist (b. 1908).

Apr 4 : Kenny Everett, British comedian (b. 1944).

Apr 4 : Priscilla Lane, American actress (b. 1915).

Apr 14 : Burl Ives, American singer and actor (b. 1909).

Apr 16 : Cy Endfield, American screenwriter (b. 1914).

Celebrity Deaths :

Apr 23 : Howard Cosell, American sportscaster (b. 1918).

Apr 27 : Willem Frederik Hermans, Dutch writer (b. 1921).

May 2 : Michael Hordern, English actor (b. 1911).

May 5 : Mikhail Botvinnik, Russian chess player (b. 1911).

May 8 : Teresa Teng, Taiwanese singer (b. 1953).

May 12 : Arthur Lubin, American film director (b. 1898).

May 12 : Adolfo Pedernera, Argentinian footballer (b. 1918).

May 14 : Christian B. Anfinsen, American chemist (b. 1916).

May 15 : Eric Porter, English actor (b. 1928).

May 18 : Elisha Cook Jr., American actor (b. 1903).

May 21 : Les Aspin, American politician (b. 1938).

May 25 : Dany Robin, French actress (b. 1927).

Celebrity Deaths :

May 26 : Friz Freleng, American animator (b. 1906).

May 29 : Margaret Chase Smith, American politician (b. 1897).

May 30 : Ted Drake, English footballer (b. 1912).

Jun 3 : J. Presper Eckert, American engineer (b. 1919).

Jun 7 : Hsuan Hua, Chinese Buddhist (b. 1918).

Jun 22 : Yves Congar, French cardinal (b. 1904).

Jun 23 : Jonas Salk, American medical researcher (b. 1914).

Jun 29 : Lana Turner, American actress (b. 1921).

Jun 30 : Georgi Beregovoi, Russian cosmonaut (b. 1921).

Jun 30 : Gale Gordon, American actor (b. 1906).

Jul 1 : Wolfman Jack, American disc jockey (b. 1938).

Celebrity Deaths :

Jul 1 : Bruce Mitchell, South African cricketer (b. 1909).

Jul 3 : Pancho Gonzales, American tennis champion (b. 1928).

Jul 4 : Bob Ross, American television painter (b. 1942).

Jul 6 : Aziz Nesin, Turkish writer (b. 1915).

Jul 13 : Ashapoorna Devi, Indian author and poet (b. 1908).

Jul 16 : Patsy Ruth Miller, American actress (b. 1904).

Jul 16 : Stephen Spender, English poet and writer (b. 1909).

Jul 17 : Harry Guardino, American actor (b. 1925).

Jul 18 : Fabio Casartelli, Italian cyclist (b. 1970).

Jul 18 : Srinagarindra, Thai princess (b. 1900).

Jul 20 : Genevieve Tobin, American actress (b. 1899).

Celebrity Deaths :

Jul 22 : Harold Larwood, British cricketer (b. 1904).

Jul 24 : George Rodger, British photojournalist (b. 1908).

Jul 25 : Charlie Rich, American singer (b. 1932).

Jul 27 : Miklós Rózsa, Hungarian composer (b. 1907).

Aug 3 : Ida Lupino, British-born American actress (b. 1918).

Aug 9 : Jerry Garcia, American guitarist (b. 1942).

Aug 11 : Phil Harris, American comedian and actor (b. 1904).

Aug 13 : Mickey Mantle, American baseball player (b. 1931).

Aug 19 : Pierre Schaeffer, French composer (b. 1910).

Aug 20 : Hugo Pratt, Italian comics creator (b. 1927).

Celebrity Deaths :

Aug 24 : Gary Crosby, American singer and actor (b. 1933).

Aug 29 : Michael Ende, German author (b. 1929).

Aug 30 : Fischer Black, American economist (b. 1938).

Sep 8 : Eileen Chang, Chinese writer (b. 1920).

Sep 12 : Jeremy Brett, English actor (b. 1933).

Sep 15 : Gunnar Nordahl, Swedish footballer (b. 1921).

Sep 29 : Madalyn Murray O'Hair, American activist (b. 1919).

Sep 29 : Pedro Nolasco, Dominican boxer (b. 1963).

Oct 5 : Pin Malakul, Thai educator and politician (b. 1903).

Oct 19 : Don Cherry, American jazz trumpeter (b. 1936).

Oct 21 : Shannon Hoon, American singer-songwriter (b. 1967).

Celebrity Deaths :

Oct 22 : Kingsley Amis, English writer (b. 1922).

Oct 22 : Mary Wickes, American actress (b. 1910).

Oct 25 : Viveca Lindfors, Swedish actress (b. 1920).

Oct 25 : Bobby Riggs, American tennis player (b. 1918).

Oct 26 : Wilhelm Freddie, Danish painter (b. 1909).

Oct 31 : Rosalind Cash, American actress (b. 1938).

Nov 4 : Gilles Deleuze, French philosopher (b. 1925).

Nov 4 : Paul Eddington, English actor (b. 1927).

Nov 7 : Ann Dunham, American anthropologist (b. 1942).

Nov 12 : Robert Stephens, English actor (b. 1931).

Nov 20 : Sergei Grinkov, Russian figure skater (b. 1967).

Nov 23 : Louis Malle, French film director (b. 1932).

Celebrity Deaths :

Nov 24 : Jeffrey Lynn, American actor (b. 1909).

Dec 2 : Robertson Davies, Canadian novelist (b. 1913).

Dec 9 : Vivian Blaine, American actress and singer (b. 1921).

Dec 18 : Nathan Rosen, Israeli physicist (b. 1909).

Dec 18 : Konrad Zuse, German engineer (b. 1910).

Dec 20 : Madge Sinclair, Jamaican-American actress (b. 1938).

Dec 22 : Butterfly McQueen, American actress (b. 1911).

Dec 22 : James Meade, English economist (b. 1907).

Dec 23 : Patric Knowles, English actor (b. 1911).

Dec 29 : Lita Grey, American actress (b. 1908).

Dec 30 : Heiner Müller, German poet and playwright (b. 1929).

Famous Leaders In 1995 :

Bill Clinton
42nd US President

John Major
British Prime Minister

Helmut Kohl
German Chancellor

Jiang Zemin
Paramount Leader of China

Popular Culture 1995 :

- Popular Films :

3 Ninjas Knuckle Up
The Amazing Panda Adventure
Bad Company
The Chicken from Outer Space
The Computer Wore Tennis Shoes
Don't Hang Up, Tough Guy!
Far from Home: The Adventures of Yellow Dog
Free Willy 2: The Adventure Home

- Popular Music :

Old Enough to Know Better
Look What the Rookie Did
Charlie Parker with Strings
Facts and Fictions
It's Five O'Clock Somewhere

Notes :

Notes :

Notes :

Notes :

Notes :

Notes :

Notes :

Notes :

Notes :

Notes :

Notes :

Notes :

Notes :

Notes :

Notes :

Notes :

Notes :

Notes :

Notes :

Notes :

Notes :

Notes :

Notes :

Notes :

Notes :

Notes :

Notes :

Notes :

Notes :

Notes :

Notes :

Notes :

Notes :

Notes :

Notes :

Notes :

Notes :

Notes :

Notes :

Notes :

Notes :

Notes :

Notes :

Notes :

Notes :

Notes :

THANK YOU

THANK YOU FOR COMPLETING OUR BOOK

YOU CAN GET MORE GREAT BOOKS OF THIS

SERIES ON OUR SHOP IN AMAZON

(VINTAGE HISTORICAL EVENTS).

DON'T FORGET TO LEAVE US A REVIEW.

WE WOULD LOVE TO HEAR YOUR

FEEDBACK OR YOUR ADIVICES

TO CREATE BETTER PRODUCTS FOR YOU.

THE END

Printed in Poland
by Amazon Fulfillment
Poland Sp. z o.o., Wrocław

54363961R00056